Spain
Hills white with snow
Stephen and Scharlie Platt

www.leveretpublishing.com

Spain: Hills white with snow
First published - January 2023
Published by Leveret Publishing
56 Covent Garden, Cambridge, CB1 2HR, UK

> Ah yes, the hills are white with snow,
> And cold with blasts that bite and freeze;
> But in the happy vale below
> The orange and pomegranate grow,
> And wafts of air toss to and fro
> The blossoming almond-trees.

Castles in Spain

By Henry Wadsworth Longfellow

ISBN 978-1-912460-663

© Stephen Platt 2024

All rights reserved. No part of this publication may be reproduced, stored in a retrieval system or transmitted in any form by any means, electronic, mechanical, photocopying, recording or otherwise, except brief extracts for the purpose of review, without the written permission of the publisher.

Spain
Hills white with snow

Sierra Nevada 1981
Mulhacén

Traverse of the Sierra Nevada

Granada

We met Maria at the Eden Dance Centre that Scharlie and I were running with our partner, Maureen Singh in the 80s. Maria was a climber and she invited us to stay with her and her parents in Granada and go climbing in the Sierra Nevada. We flew to Malaga on 1 February 1981. Unfortunately, neither of us kept a journal of the trip, so the following is constructed from memory and what we could glean from the internet.

We travelled by coach from Malaga airport and arrived at the main bus station in Granada on San Juan de Dios, from where we walked to Maria's home in the Albaicín district of the city, via the Plaza and Church of San Gil y Santa Anna. Maria lived on the Callejón Vacas and the walk was only a mile or so from the bus station.

We pass the Hamman Al Andalus, the traditional Turkish baths, before crossing the Puente Cabrera over the Rio Darro, the tributary of the River Genil we will follow to the mountains in the next days.

The Callejon Vacas is narrow and the houses offer blank walls and heavy doors on the street side, but open out within to provide splendid views

View of the Alhambra from our bedroom in the Albaicín

across the wooded ravine that guards the Alhambra and Alcazaba. Maria lives with her mother in a lovely ancient house. And her father, who is separated from her mother, lives next door. During the few days we stay with the family we pass from one house to the other enjoying their company and getting to know them. We have a lovely room with a large carved antique double bed.

The Alhambra, that we could see just across the alley from our room, was the palace and citadel of the Moorish kings and dates from 1238. It is built on an granite outcrop of the Sierra Nevada. At the western end of the rock is the Alcazaba fortress, the oldest surviving part of the Alhambra. We spent a day there site-seeing.

It was my first experience of Islamic architecture and I was bowled over. I loved the cool, light interiors, the delicate plaster work in the harem, of the Lion Palace, the glimpsed views over the Albaicín. Amazingly we learnt that the roofs rested not on stone, but on a timber frame, and that the walls were built inexpensively of rammed earth using local clay and decorated inside with gypsum plaster-work "ataujeríato to disguise the cheap construction and giving the appearance of great wealth.

View of the city from the Palace of the Lions

Plaster-work in the Palace of the Lions

We loved the paradisal garden of the Generalife, the garden of the architect in a villa next to the Alhambra palace. The water for the fountains and the rill that runs through the garden in a crisp straight line comes by aqueduct from the Darro River and from there to the Alhambra.

One evening we went to a spirited flamenco show in one of the caves only a ten minute walk down the hill on the Camino del Sacromonte, in las Cuevas los Tarantos. It was much less commercial and touristic than it appears to be today. I remember it as dark and passionate, dangerous and spirited. Maria's father explained it was a gypsy culture and that Sacromonte is the gypsy quarter of Granada. The style of flamenco is know as Zambra and is traditionally played at gypsy weddings.

Another evening Maria's father invited us to join him over a drink in his

Paradisal gardens in the Generalife

party room where he entertains his close male friends. We sit round a small circular table covered in a heavy woven mantel. It's warm, because it's an antique brazier table with a charcoal fire. Maria's father explains that the Arabic notion of "cool head, warm feet" encourages thoughtful contemplation. He also explains that the mural on the wall, of an elf-like creature riding an extended phallus was painted by one of his drinking buddies.

Church of San Gil y Santa Anna

Sierra Nevada

We caught a bus from Granada to the village of Güéjar-Sierra and from there walked along a minor road to the Barranco de San Juan, where the ravine meets the Genil River, tributary of the Guadalquivir and where the Sierra Nevada National Park starts.

The path descends to the Genil River, which is crossed by a wooden footbridge along one of the most beautiful trekking routes in Sierra Nevada. The Vereda de la Estrella walking path, that dates back to 1890 when it was built to connect Granada to the copper mines, follows a deep, wooded gorge with sensational views of the three tall peaks – The Veleta, Alcazaba and Mulhacén.

After half an hours walk we reached a big chestnut tree, known locally as the 'Grandfather' and after another half hour the path divides into two. The path left descends to the Cucaracha Hut and, further on, the Aceral Refuge. We take the direct right-hand path.

The approach continues for a couple of kilometres to reach the ruins of La Probadora mines which operated until the end of the nineteen-fifties.

Güéjar-Sierra

Further on there are other deserted mines and after an hour we reached the confluence of the Valdecasillas and Valdeinfierno Rivers where there is a wooden bridge and the path continues to the right along the Valdeinfierno River.

Soon we reach the Cueva Secreta (1.750 m), the natural bivouac under a rock where we plan to sleep. The shelter is not visible from the path, but Maria has told us how to find it. The cave is filled with dry sweet smelling straw and is warm and dry. We have good sleeping bags and a stove and food.

We stay here two nights and climb the Alcazaba on the first day and the Mulhacén on the second. Our idea is to climb to the summit, where we hope to stay the night in the refuge, and then descend into the Alpujarria the following day.

We cross the Valdeinfierno river and follow a path which traverses an ascending ridge to reach the pass of 'Majda del Palo'. From the pass we continue to the Valdecasillas river, as the path levels towards the Mulhacén.

Alcazaba (3,369 m) on left and Mulhacén (3,482 m) on right

Carving a wooden spoon because we forgot to bring one

Wooden bridge at the confluence of the Valdecasillas and Valdeinfierno Rivers

Starting the climb on the Alcazaba

Snow pitch on the Alcazaba

Upper slopes of the Alcazaba

Leaving our nest in the Cueva Secreta to climb the Mulhacén

North Face of Mulhacén via Central Couloir

The Mulhacén (3,482 m) is the highest mountain on the Iberian Peninsula and the third highest mountain in Western Europe. It is named after Abu'l-Hasan Ali, known as Muley Hacén, the penultimate Muslim ruler of Granada in the 15th century who, according to legend, was buried on the summit of the mountain.

The south flank of the mountain is gentle and presents no technical challenge. The north face of the mountain is much steeper and offers several routes involving moderately steep climbing on snow and ice (up to French grade AD) in the winter.

Our route is the Canuto Central, or central couloir, of Mulhacén's north face. It's the classic winter route of the peak, first climbed in March 1970 by Cuevas, López , Asiain, Motóse and Gómez.

The path from the Cueva steepens in a long traverse past the Chorrera de la Mosca to the plateau and the alpine lake, the Lago de la Mosca (2.895 m) from where the Mulhacén's north face is easily reached.

After 3 and a half hours from 'Cueva Secreta' the alpine lake 'de la

North faces of Alcazaba and Mulhacén

Mosca' (2.895 m) and the base of Mulhacén's north face is right in front of us.

The climb begins with easy snow slopes to reach a large debris cone at the start of the route. Once passed we continue to the left over a wide snow ledge. At the highest point of this ledge, just after the big rock-block, the 'Canuto Central' (central couloir) of the Mulhacén soars straight ahead.

We have a single 150ft rope, two dead-men (aluminium belay plates with wire loops that I hammer into the snow to protect Scharlie's ascent). We each have an ice axe, a hammer axe and crampons for our boots.

We progress up on this couloir, trying to avoid the middle to minimize stone and snow avalanches. Very soon we are at the first narrow point of the 'canuto'. It is steeper (40-45°) and the snow slope has turned to hard water ice. It's hard to get a good purchase with the axe and crampons; they only penetrate a few millimetres into the bubbly ice. At least it's thick and solid and doesn't shatter or part company with the underlying rock.

After this passage the couloir becomes wider and there is a rocky prominence which we avoid to the left. Up ahead rocks form a second

Route up Central Couloir on north face of Mulhacén

Approaching the base of the Mulhacén

An early pitch of the Mulhacén

The first steep section of the Mulhacén North face

Reaching area Laguna de la Mosca

Early pitches on the Mulhacén

Hoya de la Mosca

The Central Couloir

The crux pitch

Hard ice on the steep bit

Over the difficult section

Final snow slope

Approaching the summit

narrowing. This is the crux of the route: a difficult passage on 45-50° ice. Steve climbs it and excavates a ledge to form a stance and whacks in the dead-man plate before taking in the rope and bringing Scharlie up. That was the last difficulty of the couloir before dealing with the rocky summit block. Scharlie has been banging her axes into the ice so hard that she has grazed her knuckles and blood is seeping through her Dachstein wool mitts and leaving bright red spots on the white snow.

The third, and last part, of the ascent offers three options: snowfields to the left and right or straight up the mixed ground. We take the original route to the right over the steep snow fields to join the west ridge just before the summit. It's all fairly easy and a relief after the icy couloir.

We find the refuge, but the main part is closed and locked securely. There is a lean-to stone shelter with a couple of iron bunks with no mattresses. It's cold and bleak but we are out of the wind and will have a safe night. The wind has whipped all the snow from the summit, leaving a cap of ice so we have to keep our crampons on. All around there are piles of human excrement, from other climbers and walkers who have reached the summit over the winter. (We believe that this refuge has since

Summit

been demolished.)

The following morning we make an early start soon after dawn and head south over Mulhacén II (3,362) and begin descending into the Alpujarra.

Dusk on the summit

Loma del Mulhacén after a night spent on the summit

Las Alpujarras

The Alpujarras is a high valley system immediately south of the Sierra Nevada. It extends 60 km from Lanjaron to Ugijar and is watered by the Guadalfeo river. Snow melt means that the southern slopes of the Sierra remain green and fertile throughout the year. The area was settled by Berber people after the Moorish conquest in 711. The Al-Andalus, from North Africa, terraced the slopes and built irrigation canals, the acequia. They created small scattered villages with narrow winding streets and flat roofed houses in the style of the North African settlements they had come from. Olives are grown on the lower slopes and grapes, citrus in the valley with almond trees on the southern slopes.

The Berber people thrived here, supplying Granada with produce, until the city fell to Ferdinand and Isabella in 1492. The final Muslim revolt in the Alpujarra was crushed in 1571 and the population fell from over 40,000 to less than 7,000 by the end of the 16th century.

I knew about the Alpujarra from reading Gerald Brenan's book South of Granada about his stay in Yegen in the 20's. The book describes daily life in this small isolated village.

Mirador de Trevelez

Trevelez and terraced hillsides

Old men in a door way in Trevelez

Approaching Yegen

Acequia feeding water to Yegen

We head south along the snow covered ridge of the Loma del Tanto over the Alto del Chorrillo (2,721) to the Mirador de Trevélez. On a barren shoulder, exposed to the prevailing winds, there is a circular area of stone flags that we imagine might be used for winnowing grain. From here it's an easy walk down to Trevélaz (1,476 m) where we found somewhere to stay.

From Trevélez it was half a day's walk to Yegen following mule tracks and finally a stretch of road. We stayed in people's homes because there were no hotels or hostels in either Trevélaz or Yegen. It was winter and the hills were bare and pale brown in the weak winter sunshine. It was very peaceful and quiet here and I could imagine Gerald Brenan finding it healing after the trauma of the First World War. I think we must have got a lift back to Lanjaron to catch a bus back to Granada, or maybe there was a bus all the way.

Malaga

We went rock climbing with Maria and her friends near to Malaga. Neither of us had rock boots, but we managed a fairly easy route but bottled out of a big wall climb. Maria seconded it very elegantly and I remember her pirouetting on the tiny over hanging stance. The leader had cut his finger badly pulling on one of the bolts, so they abseiled off without completing the route.

We flew back from Malaga that evening.

Albaicín

Rock climbing in Malaga, Serranía de Ronda

Pyrenees 1987
Monte Perdido

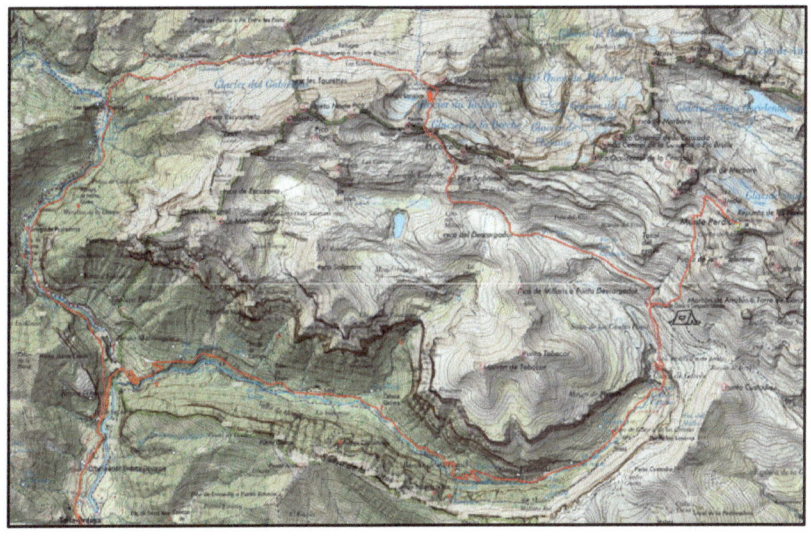

Circuit of the Parque Ordesa

Cambridge to Barcelona

Sunday 26 April 1987

Steve woke before the alarm at 5am. Scharlie stumbled downstairs, tired and feeling sick, saying "Is it worth it?". Our taxi got us to Drummer Street in plenty of time and the coach drivers were all courteous and helpful – "13 for Heathrow, 3 for Gatwick, and they're still arriving", one said, as a belated lady passenger appeared at the end of the road tugging a heavy suitcase.

Tender young leaves floating like green butterflies in the mist – I hadn't really noticed before that spring had come to Cambridge.

We had a big breakfast in the airport at Gatwick. Off with our boots and onto the baggage-check x-ray screen. .

We are two and a half hours early for the flight. Has Scharlie reformed? But she's left her new dark glasses behind at home, so not a complete

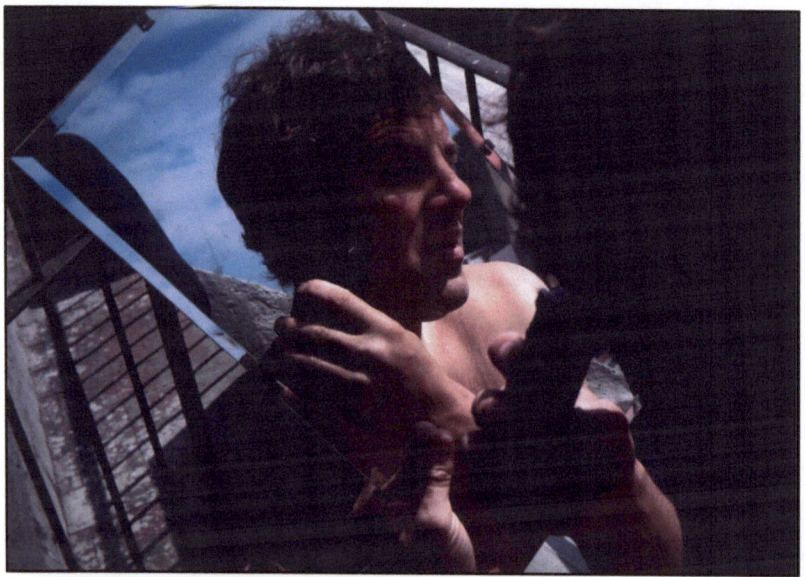

Shaving on the roof of Becky's flat

transformation! A smooth flight to Barcelona with the coast near Brighton clear, flying over the Isle of Wight, with Portsmouth in the distance.

We catch the metro to Sants station, near Ramblas, in the Ciutat Vella, the Gothic Quarter of Barcelona. From here it was a five minute walk to Portaferissa, one of the gates to the old city. Ben and Becky's flat is on the top floor with a view over alleys and tin shacks sprouting from the undulating roof-scapes. In the evening seagulls wheel in and out of the lights of the Cathedral.

We met Becky when we went to see a play at the Drama Centre next door to our home in Cambridge. The play was titled "Admiral Dubasov takes a bath". The Admiral, we learned later, was responsible for crushing rebellion and insurrection in Moscow in 1905. The company of players was called the Cambridge Experimental Theatre. Cavalry charges were performed by two men galloping across the stage on chairs. It was a most spirited performance culminating in a liberal soaking in red paint for those of the limited audience foolish enough like us to have chosen front row seats. Perhaps to make amends the two leading lights – Richard Spaul and Richard Fredman – invited us to our local, the Six Bells. There we met

Las Ramblas, Barcelona

Becky their stage manager, organiser and fixer.

Back in Barcelona, we go for a walk through the old city with Becky. Scharlie is in a strange mood, oppressed by the dark heavy buildings. Everything seems sombre, heavy, brutish and barbed; ugly without cohesion or simplicity. Her mind fills with thoughts of death, and fear of life – a conviction that she would never shake off this black weight.

Reaching the port and the open sky made her breathe easier. Steve's feet were hurting but we walked to Gaudi's Parc Guell, where there is an enormous fountain resplendent with horses and water cascades. We talked a little about our confused feelings on the way there. Nevertheless, Scharlie's spirits lift as we wander through the park. We meet Mark, Rita's artist friend, and Angela and Scharlie throws off her sombre mood. We stopped for a beer, with dire consequences for Scharlie on top of all the tea drunk at Becky's. We need a public convenience or an emergency stop at a hotel!

We are in the Plaça Nova in front of the Cathedral and Steve spots a hotel, the Hotel Colon, on the corner of Carrer del Dr. Joaquim Pou. It looks very smart, but Scharlie looks the part in her dress and jaunty hat. I

Parc Guell

wait and wait, wondering what on earth could have happened and getting increasingly concerned. What if she has had an accident or been assaulted? I'm not sure what to do. Go and find a porter, alert them at the reception or go and find out what's happening myself. I find the women's toilet and call for her. But the door is heavy and either she can't hear me or I can't hear her. So finally I try the handle and open the door. Scharlie takes up the story.

I pushed open the door and stepped into a large open room with wash basins round the perimeter. The door closed behind me and the bright light of day vanished and I was left in blackness. I could see nothing, not even my hand in front of my face. My need was urgent and finding the wall I moved along searching in increasing desperation, finally making use of

Hotel Colon

a friendly wash-basin. What a relief!

Now where was the door to escape. I kept to the security of the wall and felt my way along moving clockwise but panic set in and in the total blackness the proportions of the room expanded to the size of a football pitch and it felt as if there was no end to it and no escape. Time stopped. Then a voice "Scharlie", and a shaft of light as the door cracked open. Steve, my knight in shining armour, had tired of waiting outside in the street and had come to rescue me!

After the trauma of the afternoon, we have a relaxed supper cooked by Ben and meet Mark and Angela in Casa del Opera at 11 pm. Conversation is difficult because of noise level. Mark held the floor and we were happy to be quiet and listen.

We visit the Centre Excursionista de Catalunya. It's not just a hiking club. It was founded during the time of the Catalan resistance at the end of the 19th century and was instrumental in preserving and promoting the Catalan language. It's at the top of a flight of stone stairs in a beautiful colonnaded building with stained glass windows. The columns are from a Roman temple that stood on the Monte Tabor and were removed and

Mercat St Josep, La Boqueria

incorporated in the medieval building that the centre has occupied since 1902. Luckily we find someone who knows all about climbing Monte Perdido and can give us advice. He suggests we get a bus to Torla and walk to the Goriz hut, from where we can climb the mountain easily in a day. He warns us about the dangers of the ascent, of which later, and suggest that we then do a round trip back to Torla via the Roland Gap and Bujaruelo.

Centre Excursionista de Catalunya

Barcelona to Huesca

Monday 27 April 1987

Scharlie wakes, her body heavy with sleep but her mind refreshed. The blackness of the day before has gone and she sees people going about their business like anywhere else – detail variety light and shade, movement and human faces to immerse yourself in watching, suspend introspection, be an eye.

Lunch in the station cafe. Steve asks, "shall we live here – you get a job gardening in the build-up to the Olympic Games. Perhaps a position for me in the University".

We catch the Metro to Passeig de Gràcia then a train to Lerida. At the rail station we take a taxi down a long dry street to the bus station. We find a cafe in a cool alley where we can shelter from the rain. We discuss intuition, whether one should rely on it or not, how often it's wrong etc.

Las Ramblas

We buy a raffle ticket from a waiter and watch a cycle race on the TV.

After an hour or so we take the bus to Barbastro. On the bus, Steve talks to a former American chef who is returning home soon. He talks about the world being full of disaster, but has twinkling eyes.

We get helpful advice to continue on the bus to Huesca and stop the night there and get an early morning bus to Sabinanigo. In Huesca we find a taxi to take us to the Hostel Centro, not surprisingly in the centre of Huesca. We have a clean room with bathroom plus a two course meal with drink and coffee for £10 in nearby cafe. In general, people here seem courteous and friendly.

Hostel El Centro, Huesca

Huesca to Torla

Tuesday 28 April 1987

We catch the 10 am bus to Torla and get lunch in the restaurant "Banjo Mas Arriba". An odd looking couple say an extremely long grace. To relax and pass the time, we take a short walk beside river Ara up the valley to Cota Yuero. We miss the path and follow the road for the last bit. Steve's boots, his Galibier Hivernale double boots, which he bought 15 years ago to climb high mountains in the Andes are all he has. They are most uncomfortable walking on the road and hurt his shins. We are both feeling unfit.

We drink a coffee at the local restaurant then camp behind bushes, where the sign says "it's forbidden to camp". We sleep from 10pm to 9am. Lichen whitening the trunks of pine trees. Mauve Alpine Soldanella popping through the turf; white snow-capped peaks towering above us.

Torla

Parque Ordesa

Torla to Refugio Goriz   13km

Wednesday 29 April 1987

We start late at 11am to walk to the Refugio Goriz, following a broad path that gently rises up the spectacular Ordesa Valley. It's slightly too early for spring flower spikes. We reach the Puente de los Navarros where the path turns from north to east, through the Bosque de Turieto and passes the Cascadas de Arripas,

Before we begin the steeper climb to the refuge, we pass the Grados de Soasa and Cascada de la Cola de Caballo on the Rio Arazas. For last two miles to the hut the path follows a steep zigzag up the rock wall and then a tramp across a snow slope. We camp on a rocky platform above the refuge with a splendid view along the steep cliffs of Las Tres Sorores that border the canyon below Monte Perdido. We plan to climb the mountain tomorrow.

Cascada Grados de Soasa

MONTE PERDIDO

Monte Perdido (3,355 m) is the highest peak in the Ordesa National Park and the third highest peak in the Pyrenees. The "La Escupidera" stretch from Lago Helado the Frozen Lake (2980 m) to the summit (3355 m) has sadly been the scene of many accidents, the majority of which were fatal. More than fifty climbers have died here, nearly all when the gully was snow-covered. In summer, when the snow has melted, there is an easy zig-zag scree strewn path.

The icy slope is steep with an exit to the left before the final summit slope, and if anyone loses their footing and is unable to stop their slide down the snow slope, they fall over steep cliffs. Hence the name La Escupidera, which means spittoon, implying that the mountain literally spits the mountaineer into the void. Luis Masgrau, President of the Aragonese Mountaineering Federation (FAM) said, "It is without a doubt the most dangerous place in the Aragonese Pyrenees".

We didn't know about the death toll at the time and we found it relatively easy and just needed to be careful, especially on the descent, not to catch ones crampons in ones gaiters and trip as we weren't roped.

Monte Perdido and the route up "La Escupidera"

Puente de la Ereta, confluence of Rio Ara and Rio Arazas

Cascada Cola de Caballo

Our camp above the Goriz hut

Starting out to climb Monte Perdido

Climbing Monte Perdido

Thursday 30 April 1987

It's a cold, clear night and the turf is frozen hard at 9am when we set off. This means that the snow is firm enough not to sink past our ankles. We contour around, looking for lake as marker point to climb the ridge before realising that the lake is invisible under a cover of snow.

We follow the footsteps of climbers who are three quarters of an hour ahead of us until we reach a large rock where we rest a moment to don our crampons for the steeper slope and the "zona de accidentes" mentioned in the guide. If you slip here you go a long way! Scharlie concentrated hard and only got the faintest collywobbles where the snow hardened to ice near the summit at 3,355 m. We made summit in four hours.

We met another climber on our descent. He had two axes and Scharlie thought that she would have been glad of two too. Steve calmly talked her down the steep bit, "Keep your feet widely spaced and use your axe as a third leg. If you slip, whack that ice axe straight, in no messing about. Roll onto you tummy and remember to keep your feet up; you'll cartwheel if your crampons dig in.

We stop for lunch at 2pm on a flat rock halfway down and get back to the tent by 3:30pm, before it gets dark. There is a change-over of guardians at the refuge, and the new team offer us a "free cup of coffee for the English". Dropping off in our sleeping bags in the tent, birds are making a noise like the rustling of a paper bag.

Cylindro de Marboré in the background

Beginning "La Escupidera", the Spittoon

Ascent of the "La Escupidera"

Summit of Monte Perdido

Dscending carefully to avoid tripping

On the descent

Summit of Monte Perdido

Back safe at our tent

Refugio Sarradets via Brèche de Roland

Friday 1 May 1987

We pack the tent and set off at 10.30. The walking is easy across rocky slabs and wide snowfields with peaks flowing up on every side. After an hour the snow softens and it is troublesome wading through it. We keephigh under the cliffs to have less climbing. We stop and watch a couple of climbers tackling the rock face above us. They have come over on skis, which they have left stuck in the snow. We reach a rock cave within sight of the gap with a tricky icy dissent without crampons, since we can't be bothered to stop and put them on. We reach the Brèche de Roland at 2pm

At the gap a party of cross-country skiers come through having climbed up from the French side. We stop and sunbathe, waiting for tea to brew. On the descent to Refugio Sarradets we sink to the crotch in soft snow and only make progress with a kind of sideways wallowing. You spend five minutes digging out one leg and eventually resort to canoeing down on your side using an elbow as an oar. Oh for skis, to ski down elegantly!.

We decide to stay at the refuge and start early tomorrow when the snow is hard in the morning. We strip off and sunbathe on the roof. The refuge fills up with bank-holiday makers. Our food is running low and other people's crusty French bread looks mouthwatering. We get to bed at 8pm. The bunk-room is freezing and full of snorers but in the middle of the night we are sweating so profusely we shed most of our clothes.

Traversing westwards

Warm in the winter sunshine

Stop for a quick break

Approaching the Brèche de Roland

Descending snow slope from the Brèche de Roland to the Sarradets hut

Refugio Sarradets to Torla via Bujaruelo   9.5km

Saturday 2 May 1987

People stir about 6am while it's still dark. Looking out through the window the steep slope up to the pass was full of skiers as if on a zigzag ladder. We get up after the main rush at 6.30, finish the last of our porridge and leave by 8am. The mountain soft pink and blue in the morning light. The initial slope down from the pass is very steep but there are good footsteps so although the snow is hard and slightly slippy, we manage with ice axes without needing to fix our crampons.

We follow a long traverse, contouring round with cliffs to our left, avoiding the deep valley leading down to Gavarnie on our right. We follow the ski tracks and meet lots of parties coming up, mostly saying "Bonjour". The snow is slightly softening and we are glad we left early. Above us on the cliffs there are various parties ice climbing.

Scharlie outside the Refuge de Sarradets

We decide that cross-country skiing is definitely worth investigating. It's slightly slower than walking uphill, but amazing coming down! To turn on an uphill slope you have to put your feet into first position ballet and lift the skis right round.

At the pass called the Puerta de Bujarelo there is a notice in French saying that we are at the frontier and will have to pass a customs post. But there doesn't seem to be any sign of one. The road to the pass, that was originally planned in Napoleon's time, has only been built on the French side. On the Spanish side there is a track, snow-covered until we reach the tree line – pine, beech and spring flowers of primula, anemone and dicentra. We reach Bujaruelo at 11:30am where the Aduana and Church in Bujarelo are in ruins. Only a large house used as a restaurant remains

Heading towards Bujarelo

Leaving the Sarradets Hut

Puente de Bujarelo

Barcelona

3 May – 6 May 1987

We spent our last two days in Barcelona site seeing. We visit Montjuic, the Jewish Hill, and ride the cable car to the top but our main focus is to see some of the work of Antoni Guadi, Catalan architect (1852-1926).

   La Casa Milà (La Pedrera), with its white stone curves and sculptural roofscape and the Casa Batlló fish-skull balconies and gorgeous mosaics,

Gaudi's Casa Batlló

both on the Passeig de Gràcia. We catch the 24 bus to the Parque Güell, Concrete tree trunks hold up the promenade and the sinuous mosaic benches look like exotic snakes.

Most amazing of all his still unfinished masterpiece, the Sagrada Familia cathedral. In 1987 the four Apostles Towers were still under construction but amazingly you were allowed inside to climb the perilous and narrowing spiral staircase inside. A party of chubby school girls were descending as we climbed up and we were pushed outwards at each of the open stone window opening that circled the tower.

We fly home on Wednesday the 6 May.

Gaudi's Sagrada Familia

When one looks south from Granada across the red towers of the Alhambra one sees a range of mountains known as the Sierra Nevada which have snow on them all the year round. This is the famous view, so endlessly reproduced on picture postcards, which brings the tourist to Andalusia in the spring. But forget the Alhambra, forget the nightingales, and consider only the mountains. They are high enough to boast of having small glaciers, and if you cross them you will come to a broad, hollow country, very broken and separated from the sea by a coastal range. It is this country, which till quite recently could only be explored on foot or mule-back, that is the subject of this book. Or rather the subject is a village, by name Yegen, that lies within it. It is a poor village, one of the poorest of the eighty or so that stud the Alpujarra, as this fertile region is called, and it stands high above the sea. It is so remote that until the present road was built it took two days to reach it from Granada. But in its primitive way it is beautiful, and since I lived there for some six or seven years between 1920 and 1934 and took an interest in its affairs, I feel that I know enough to write at some length about it. The principal part of this book then is devoted to an account of this village, with its customs, its folk-lore, its festivals, and a certain number of its more striking characters with their quarrels and love affairs.

Gerald Brenan, *South from Granada*, 1957

www.ingramcontent.com/pod-product-compliance
Lightning Source LLC
Chambersburg PA
CBHW041803160426
43191CB00001B/20